AF282557

Janine Bray-Mueller
Le Haut Quérant
56120 Pleugriffet, France
www.braymueller.com

Book Layout ©2013 BookDesignTemplates.com
Book cover (CC0 Creative Commons) by Pixaline from Pixabay
Dandelion Balloon image (CC0 Creative Commons) by Comfreak from Pixabay

Manufactured and published by BoD-Books on Demand, Norderstedt, Germany
Evidence of Proof—Testimonials / Janine Bray-Mueller
1st Ed.
ISBN 978-3-757810900

Evidence of Proof
Testimonials

METHODS FOR COLLECTING TESTIMONIALS

Step-by-Step Practical Advice for Freelance Teachers

Janine Bray-Mueller

Production and Publishing
BoD–Books on Demand, Norderstedt
ISBN 978-3-757810900

Bibliografische Information der Deutschen
Nationalbibliotek:
Die Deutsche Nationalbibliothek verzeichnet diese
Publikation in der Deutschen Nationalbibliografie;
detaillierte bibliografische Daten sind im Internet über
http://dnb.dnb.de abrufbar.

Deutsche Nationalbibliotek bibliographic information:
The German National Library lists this publication in the
Deutsche Nationalbibliografie; Detailed bibliographic data
are available on the Internet at http://dnb.dnb.de.

Manufactured and published by: BoD - Books on Demand,
Norderstedt, Germany

ISBN 978-3-757810900

QUICK READS FOR BUSY FREELANCERS

Contents

Evidence of Proof—*Testimonials*

METHODS FOR COLLECTING TESTIMONIALS

Step-by-Step Practical Advice for Freelance Teachers

Janine Bray-Mueller

Preface

During the first two-thirds of my working life (the late 70s, 80s and early 90s), I never gave testimonials a single thought. The idea of being a full-time, one-person business owner (like we do today) would not have been feasible. Without the digital tools we take for granted today, a freelance teaching career was a daunting prospect. Today, however, the possibilities are wide open.

I was no exception and forced myself through various long (computer-related) learning curves.

However, it was *marketing* my little business that kept me financially afloat. And one factor was testimonials. They saved me a lot of time, frustration, and energy in persuading future customers to enrol in my English language courses.

Did I know why I wanted testimonials? Back then, not really. But today, I know differently and understand much more clearly the benefits of collecting testimonials, and that's why I wrote this book.

Why collect testimonials?

Should you make an effort to get testimonials?

Yes, because they can make or break your freelancing business.

1. Testimonials (a marketing tool) enable you to catch the interest of new students.

2. Testimonials reveal information about your teaching service that only clients and students can speak about.

3. You can steer your testimonials to close information gaps in your promotional materials.

4. When your students are satisfied with your courses, testimonials give them a chance to show their appreciation. So please don't take away their opportunity to express their gratitude for a wonderful and satisfying experience.

5. Testimonials are an endorsement that your clients made a good decision by investing in *you*.

6. Testimonials can be used for reversing risks—the worries and doubts—potential customers feel when they enrol for the first time.

Creating credibility with testimonials

As teaching business owners, we need to recognise that testimonials gain credibility for our teaching services. They prove that other students have paid our (higher) fees and have enjoyed attending our courses. When testimonials are voluntarily given, they are one of the most valuable tools we can possess to attract—and catch—new customers.

Should you go through all this hassle every time?

The answer is *yes*, for three reasons:

1. Clients and students are explaining insights about your course, lesson, or product. This gives *you* an idea about the students' experience in the lesson or workshop. Ten participants will provide ten different insights of your business because no participant will have the same point of view.

2. A student's or customer's experience increases each time they attend your courses or read or use a teaching product. Their growing expertise means that our courses have to meet these new expectations. So we need to capture them as well.

3. New observations help us improve our tuition and teaching products. When we implement the requested (or implied) changes, we strengthen our teaching service exponentially.

Have you read a good book that kept you sleepless until you finished it? And a friend asks you what you thought about it? You'd probably go into a fair amount of detail about what you liked about the book, how it was a page-turner, etc.

In other words, you gave a testimonial when your friend asked you for one.

You feel great when another person receives or uses that information. The same happens when you recommend an excellent restaurant or a film worth seeing. The feeling-great part is the reason we give recommendations. People like to do this frequently.

It's the same feeling when we ask our customers for a testimonial. They don't see it as a favour but a means to pass on excellent recommendations to others—our colleagues or strangers.

Don't be surprised when the requested testimonials become wordy (i.e., meaty). You should, in fact, dance with glee and be happy because these are worth their weight in gold.

A former student's recommendation will revoke doubts by defusing suspicions about the *quality* of tuition you offer.

Readers recognise authenticity when they read them. And rightly so. They make decisions based on what they read. For example, their indecision fades away when they read other people stating they have made the right decision by investing in your courses.

You may not use all of them immediately for various reasons. However, collecting as many as you can is still worth your while.

Testimonials are teaching freelancers' best friends and supporters because they help us to grow our teaching business by:

- Finding new students
- Supporting our prices and lesson rates
- Qualifying the quality of our tuition

Testimonials as risk-reversal tools

Eliminating student and customer worries

Potential customers are reluctant because they are plagued by past experiences. They are also guided by *their* own perceptions of tuition and teaching services (regardless of which teaching field). They have at least three reasons why they *won't* enrol in your courses:

1. First, they are constantly tapping in the dark about tuition quality. Quite a few potential customers are wary because they've suffered unpleasant experiences in the past.

2. Second, they want to know whether they can attain their (learning) objectives. They've tried before but failed. So why will it work this time—with you?

3. Third, potential customers want to gauge the risk factors involved. Is it worth the cost? What if they realise they don't like your teaching method? What

happens then? What if something happens and they must change their learning plans (private or in their job)?

Unless you have a plan in place for recommendations and referral requests from your satisfied clients (testimonials), you stand to lose many future customers.

Here is an example of such a plan using three steps:

Step 1:

We need to prepare a list of typical student problems and obstacles. We can start by asking one of our **preferred students**[1] to list problems that plagued them in the past (before they attended our courses). Alternatively, we can prepare a list of problems and obstacles we know persistently hinder students from enrolling in our courses. These hindrances are the ones that need to be defused in our promotional materials.

Step 2: We allow the preferred student to choose one obstacle or problem (over all others mentioned) from the list elicited in Step 1. As an alternative, we pick the most pressing obstacle we believe needs to be fully explained and resolved as soon as possible for our teaching service.

---

[1] **Preferred students:** For an explanation, please see the chapter on Terminology used in this book.

Step 3: We ask one (or more) of our students to give us a testimonial referring to the chosen obstacle or problem.

And in practice:

Earlier, we mentioned three problems (i.e., Steps 1 + 2 have already been carried out):

1. **Problem/Obstacle: The student didn't like the teacher and their teaching methods**

   When a student's past experience is the primary obstacle, we first contact past students who have enjoyed our classes and teaching methods. Afterwards, we ask them to relate their past versus current experience with us (you) as their teacher and compare it to past experiences.

2. **Problem/Obstacle: The student never achieved their learning objectives**

   Let's assume the student's unsuccessful experience (in achieving their learning goals) is the primary obstacle. We get in touch with past students who successfully reached their self-determined learning objectives. We ask them to relate their experience with us and how our course (or courses) fundamentally helped them achieve their predetermined goals.

3. Problem/Obstacle: The student wonders whether the course is worth the money and their time

We should get in touch with similarly worried (past) students and ask them to testify why taking our courses was a good investment of their time and money.

What happens to those other obstacles or problems sitting on your list?

We use them for new testimonials, of course. But first, you must take care of your priorities—the primary obstacle or problem takes prime space in your promotional materials.

Testimonials are fantastic written examples you use to educate potential students. They provide the *whats*, the *hows*, the *where* and *when* you teach. The answers will quieten customers' lurking worries about past (bad?) experiences. In addition, they provide proof that your asking price and teaching methods are justifiable, so they won't quibble at your prices.

How? Because testimonials are documented *third-party* proof of the nature and excellence of your tuition.

Yes, most customers want the proclaimed service to be given professionally and efficiently—in just the manner described on your website or promotional teaching materials. But, at the same time, they are looking for **proof** that your teaching service can provide it. Reading testimonials from past students helps them assess their doubts and worries about satisfaction—an understandable risk when considering unknown services.

Consequently, when asking for testimonials from our students, we should ensure two aspects—the students' **past experience** and the students' **current perception.** We must ensure these are present in the testimonials wherever we can. These two aspects answer potential customer objections towards your teaching service that would otherwise prevent them from enrolling (that's when they say: *Yes, but...*). Testimonials must remove whatever doubt causes their reluctance to take that last step.

There is a hook, however. Testimonials and referrals must *sound* authentic and genuine.

They are only believable when *you* are not praising your own teaching service. Instead, these should unmistakably represent satisfied customer references (i.e., recall how you would describe a good book, restaurant or film to a friend).

Another positive side-effect is that they are also useful for you as the owner of your teaching business. They can be employed as a tool for feedback to improve your teaching service. (Testimonials as feedback will be explained later in the book.)

Testimonials help students to accept (higher) prices

Feedback and testimonial referrals help make our teaching service attractive for new customers, but how do these reflect (testify) price acceptance?

The truth is there is no difference in how we compare prices when choosing a plumber, an electrician, or any other specialist. The general steps we undertake are:

- We ask our circle of friends and colleagues whom they would recommend.

- Then we check their written testimonials and feedback on their websites.

Sugary-sweet testimonials

The convincing tone of a written reference will impress potential students. However, when they sound too sugary-sweet, they sound false, raising suspicions in the reader, and they won't invest in your courses.

Over-persuasive language or vague niceties won't convince potential students either. Instead, they must contain 'hand-and-foot' details that ring both true and convincing.

- This 'ring of conviction' will persuade new students to hire you (and no other teacher).

- The number of testimonials indirectly proves these satisfied students paid your asking price and were happy to do so.

So, let's not forget to ask our customers to provide them.

The story of a false testimonial

All testimonials are useful, but sometimes they may not be what you want nor produce the results you expect, particularly when they are based on an untruth.

A false testimonial born out of pride, deceit, and greed when in a moment of despair, a miller's father extolled in public how his daughter could spin straw into gold. The news spread until it came to the ears of the king.

As a result, the king marries the miller's daughter and forces her to spin straw into gold, which, of course, she cannot.

The consequences were almost dire for the king and queen and their heir apparent—were it not for a lucky chance. And so the fairy tale ends happily, albeit with a moral warning in disguise.

The example above is a German tale (Brothers Grimm) about Rumpelstiltskin (a self-seeking and evil dwarf). It demonstrates how such a **false** testimonial almost loses the next heir to a throne in a fairy tale.

Yes, testimonials *feel* problematic because they raise real-world issues. In addition, they *are* problematic because many teachers prefer word-of-mouth referrals rather than written recommendations or standard types of feedback-cum-testimonial.

The problem with spoken referrals is that they can be refuted. On the other hand, testimonial referrals are less likely to be questioned because they are (documented) *third-party* proof. As such, they are more readily accepted.

Using testimonials to solve problems

This may sound curious, but I've yet to meet a teaching colleague who recognises testimonials as a *problem-solving tool.*

Book-writing authors know there are no new story ideas. So, an author must combine recurring 'old' ideas with fresh slants to write new stories in new books.

Similarly, our students and customers are facing no new or unique problems. They are all, in fact, *recurring* problems.

There are no 'new' problems

Problems in getting testimonials isn't a *new* problem. It's a *recurring* problem, and it's a recurring problem because it continuously repeats itself by many people worldwide in all businesses (commercial, industrial, educational, etc.).

So why not address it by its proper name and present 'the problem' as the one only *you* can solve in your teaching service?

Stating the problem

For example, how many participants would raise their hands if you were to give a presentation and ask this question?

> *Who wants to know how to get longer and better-quality testimonials from their students?*

You may expect a few participants to raise their hands, but not many.

This question doesn't describe a problem. It presents a solution—*longer and better-quality testimonials*. It doesn't define a specific problem, and certainly not one that raises doubts in the participants' heads. Instead, the question presents a *nice-to-have* solution at best. They would think: *Yes, that would be nice.*

For comparison, let's change the wording in this question and consider how many participants would raise their hands when we tweak the question and reword it like this:

> *Who would like to know how to persuade their students to give longer and better-quality testimonials?*

I believe quite a few participants would raise their hands because the second question describes a specific problem (*getting longer and better-quality student testimonials*). **But it also provokes** the participants to:

1. **Mentally** tick the box that they already have them, only to then start wondering: *Are they good enough?*

2. Wonder **why** they should have them (i.e., *meaty* testimonials)

3. Wonder **how** they can even get them in the first place

What's happening? The participants are now **engaged** emotionally, especially when they realise they have a gap in their knowledge.

This is no longer a *nice-to-have* solution but a growing awareness of missing answers. It creates a situation that is no different to our potential clients when they read the glowing texts most teaching services offer.

Solve the recurring problem

Once we've chosen a 'problem' to resolve, we must create the contrast and ask our testimonial-givers to present 'the solution' to defuse the issue. And this brings us to the next point. How do we avoid the *sameness* everyone else writes as 'their solution'?

This book tackles this issue. How to get testimonials that provide individual angles to a single problem by describing how your courses resolved it for them.

Adieu regurgitated testimonials.

Testimonials are documented third-party proof

Documented testimonials and referrals written by your students are **physical proof of satisfaction**. They provide evidence about the quality and professionalism of your teaching service.

How do documented testimonials help in finding new students?

New customers know neither you nor the quality of your tuition. In fact, they are confronted with at least **three** questions about your teaching business:

1. Why should they hire *you* (your teaching service)?

2. Your teaching methodology and niches

3. What proof can you provide?

Testimonials produced by satisfied customers provide proof, especially when your prices are in the higher bracket range of your teaching field.

> NOTE: When important decisions are made, the *price question* is frequently overlooked.

Potential customers aren't interested in upsetting the apples from your apple cart—your tuition or teaching products. They want to know, instead, how each apple tastes before biting into it themselves.

This means they are looking for the *'before'* and *'after'* situations of individual students—details of true stories told by others who have experienced your courses.

They want to know about your teaching method and the teaching materials used, how you run the lessons or courses, the digital media tools used, and how difficult or helpful these were.

They also want information about the teacher:

- *How flexible was the instructor?*

- *How flexible is the teacher when lessons have to be postponed and rescheduled?*

- *Was the instructor good at explaining things?*

  And an apple cart holds a lot of apples.

Testimonials as a referral system

Most future customers don't choose a private instructor by investing a lot of their time in detailed research (online or offline). Instead, as we know, they prefer to follow a referral route.

You may have the best teaching service in the world. Still, you must provide examples of how others describe your teaching service and evidence of excellence—an evaluation and review. This means you need to arrange a testimonial referral system to collect *third-party proof* references.

You may prefer to concentrate on getting new customers by telling them all about your courses, lessons, and workshop-seminars. But...

- **Future students and clients WANT to know pertinent details describing your teaching service methods** from people who have *already participated* in them.

- **Future students' and clients'** interest lies purely in reports **describing other students'** *experience, experience,* and *even more of their experience.*

What if you don't have any testimonials (yet)?

Don't be like the queen in the Rumpelstiltskin fairy tale and give in to despair because of her father's false testimonial. These inevitably cause disastrous consequences. Be upfront and honest with your first students. Ask them for a testimonial after a few lessons. You will find that they are more than ready to provide you with that (coveted) testimonial.

Three lessons (or a day's instruction) suffice to convince students about the quality and style of your work.

But...

What kinds of testimonials should you focus on first?

Because you don't have any—yet.

Base your first testimonials on two different information sources: *logistical* questions or *experience-based* questions (see p. 41).

Until you gain more experience collecting testimonials, I propose your first testimonials are based on *logistical-*question topics.

1. The logistics of the course being offered, or

2. In answering questions about the course itself and its instructor, i.e., yourself

Logistical questions about the teaching business

Typical logistical questions are about the courses. For example, *language course* questions often asked are:

- How much does private tuition cost?

- Are the courses face-to-face or online? One-to-one or in small groups?

- How much time do I need to plan for learning (or refreshing)? How many lessons will I need?

- How often do lessons or classes take place?

- Will homework be involved?

Logistical questions about the course instructor

And then, questions emerge from *past* learning experiences, such as how experienced is the tutor? Has the tutor qualifications in the subject area I need to resolve my career issues (or other personal reasons)?

- What is the teacher like?

- How does the teacher carry out their courses (lessons)?

- I'm a slow learner. Will the teacher be patient enough?

- I learn quickly. Will the teacher be able to provide enough material to hold my interest?

These questions are reproduced to show you that queries exist *subconsciously* and that potential customers want answers with the least fuss.

A freelancer who provides testimonials answering these subconscious questions wins the customer's confidence because they provide *third-party* proof.

A testimonial is just a testimonial, isn't it?

First, let us discuss what does *not* immediately come to mind when talking about testimonials, namely pictures and photos.

Images are not strictly spoken or written testimonials. However, images still represent *your* teaching service. So go ahead. Look at the photos and graphics (on your website and social media pages) and observe whether they convey the **teaching reputation** (*brand*) you want to achieve for your service.

What sense will your visitors feel when they glance at your teaching service (promotional materials, website, and social media pages)? When you want to add *fun*, do these images portray an overall fun element? Are students enjoying themselves? Do example worksheets illustrate fun assignments?

Do you want your service to express a distinctive sense of seriousness? Or convey professionalism? Perhaps your aim is to show pictures of what your students have attained as achievements or milestones in their learning careers?

Testimonials aren't simply testimonials because they must carry out a specific job. They are multifunctional beasts of burden.

The first realisation is that testimonials perform at least two functions. In whatever form they eventually reappear as testimonials, they are not purely 'recommendations' *per se*.

The purpose of testimonials

Testimonials fill in gaps—the missing information about your teaching service. As these are written by a third party, they have more weight; the ring of truth.

Such testimonials present the *credibility* we need as they provide *proof of our expertise.*

The second function has a weightier job to accomplish.

The job to be done

The visionary innovation consultant Clay Christensen[2] called this second function a *'job to be done'*, a theory based on the fact that people 'hire' a product or service to do a specific job.

---

[2] Clayton Magleby Christensen (*1952 †2020) was an American academic and business consultant who developed the theory of 'disruptive innovation.'

> ## Clay Christensen's theory: *The job that has to be done*
>
> **(1) When « ... »,   (2) I want to « ... »,   (3) so I can « ... »**
>
> 1. **When** *refers to the situation that causes a potential customer to start a search for freelance teachers*
>
> 2. **I want to** *refers to the customer's motivation*
>
> 3. **So I can** *refers to the outcome (the customer's ultimate aim whether it is a learning aim or a private or business goal)*

The testimonial also has a *job-to-be-done* function
—it has a purpose—

Once entrepreneurial freelancers know what job customers want to accomplish, they can home in on it by requesting testimonials that support '*the job to be done*' from past students.

- Testimonials connect a purpose to *the core problem or a strong wish* (the WIIFM factor[3]) *students want to resolve.*

I discovered a story written in 2008 by Derek Sivers[4] explaining how to sell *music* by solving a specific problem or wish, similar to Clay Christensen's 'disruptive innovation' theory.

---

[3] **WIIFM:** See chapter on *Terminology used in this book* for an explanation

[4] Derek Sivers: https://bit.ly/SB_candle

The candlemaker story

In his article, Derek Sivers asks the reader to imagine two candle makers:

> One says, "My candles have only the finest wax with the best quality wick!"
>
> The other says, "These are prayer candles. Light one whenever you pray."
>
> There are dozens of people who will buy the first. But millions who will buy the second.

Why does one candlemaker sell more than the other?

The first candlemaker claims to only use the finest wax with the best quality wick in his candles and sells a few dozen candles.

- He sold his candles using solely *features*—the finest wax with best quality wick.

The second candlemaker, however, made no claims to quality. He made *prayer* candles for people to light while they prayed. Unlike the first candlemaker, even though the wax and wick quality was not as good, he sold 'millions' of candles.

- He sold his candles using a *benefit* to touch people's emotions, people who want to use the candles. He gave them a *purpose* to buy his candles.

The framework is simple

A purpose (partnered with an emotional benefit) helps students choose one teaching service over others. The purpose clearly describes how to fulfil a specific purpose that answers potential students' questions: *Why this particular teaching service? What will it do for me? How will it help me achieve « … »?*

The question is, what purpose—the job—should each testimonial answer? And in what format?

Spoilt for choice

When people think about testimonials, they think of *written testimonials.* But, unfortunately, this assumption isn't quite correct.

Sometimes thoughts should be given to how people with *disabilities* may prefer to give or receive testimonials.

Testimonials come in many formats, leading to another little-known fact. Our future (potential) customers prefer a *choice* of media mediums concerning giving (and receiving) testimonials. We have to consider their preferences when planning our strategies for getting them. For example, there are groups of people:

- Who cannot or prefer not to write one because they suffer from one or other forms of neurodivergent disorders (e.g., ADHD, dyslexia, or autism).

These people often prefer to give and listen to **audio** and **video** testimonials.

- With *hearing disabilities*: These people may choose to give **written** testimonials but occasionally provide **video** testimonials instead. The same can be said for *technically inclined* people.

- Who may **not** have disabilities but juggle their busy lives (career and private), trying to fit in everything they want to do. Despite their willingness, they are just too busy and preoccupied to sit down and think about what to write. People in this group would find it easier to **dictate** testimonials **using a recording app on their mobile telephones.**

TIP: Have you given thought how your potential students' preferred method to give testimonials already provide clues as to the type of learner they are? Just ask them which kind of testimonials they prefer most. *Record on their mobiles? Videos? Written?*

As teachers, we are aware of the six main learning skills and how they affect learning:

- Tactile-Kinaesthetic Learners (touch)

- Auditory Learners (hear)

- Visual Learners (see)

- Verbal Learners (speech/writing)

- Analytic Learners (technology and data)

- Global (inter- and intrapersonal, cultural behaviours)

Resistance towards testimonials

Is it reluctance or procrastination?

What if *the customer* feels reluctant to write or record a testimonial? Not everyone is eager to write or record testimonials. It's another 'boring chore', or they don't have the time to carry out your request.

The first sign is when the student procrastinates and makes excuses: '*Oh, sorry, there was so much to do in the office, I didn't have time.*' Have you heard these typical excuses where they'll try to convince you they will write one next week?

What is *really* going on here?

Nine out of ten cases are when people have gone blank when they see a sheet of white paper (or a blank screen) and don't know what to write. They feel it is too complicated. They don't know what to write. So, perhaps, a telephone call may be the solution. You can both step away from the wording of their testimonials by letting the students rattle off the answers as you ask them questions orally.

The tenth case is when the student is unhappy about your tutoring and doesn't want to write a negative testimonial— a different problem altogether.

What holds *you* back from asking for testimonials?

What if it is *you* who feels awkward asking questions? How do you find the *braveness* to ask them? How do any of us feel brave enough to approach our students and ask them for one?

It's amazing how the majority of us are frightened of this process. It's not that we don't believe in ourselves. Instead, we just worry about whether we are good enough to ask for testimonials. Then, when we convince ourselves that we can, we worry about whether we can obtain *useable* testimonials from interviews (whether on the telephone or face-to-face).

So yes, most of us will always struggle to ask and get testimonials. And then, how do we overcome our inner beast? By following a plan. After all...

Preparation is the key

Write down the questions you would like to use. (These can be found in the chapters on pages 41, 71 and 79.) You'll need different testimonials referring to various aspects of your tuition and your teaching service offer. In addition to proving your teaching quality, you will also need the rapport between you and your students and how they achieved their (learning) objectives.

Your aim is to fill in all information holes where you feel uncomfortable when 'boasting' about your abilities—but believe potential students would like to have the information.

- If you'd like a testimonial explaining why your students first decided against enrolling (but then did and were glad they did), ask them: *Why?* And then ask them: *What changed their minds?*

- If you'd like a testimonial detailing how a student's success led to a promotion, prompt them for their story of how your lessons helped them achieve their promotion.

- Suppose you want testimonials detailing why students decide to come to your lessons and later become repeat students. You can ask them how their previous learning experiences compare against their new experience (in your course).

The more your students understand you want *their story— their experiences*—the fewer monosyllabic, short and boring answers you'll receive (see p. 56; the *before* and *after* situations).

Some examples for preparing suggestive questions

- Primary reasons why students are taking or attending a course, workshop or seminar

- Decisions made by potential students before (and when) considering courses, workshops or seminars

- Requests on how to improve courses, workshops or seminars

- Requests for stories about experiences and results of taking a course, workshop or seminar

- Advice to future participants

- Anything else students would like to say or to add?

No time to prepare testimonials

When online students don't have time to prepare their testimonials, talk to them to elicit their feelings about preparing a testimonial as part of their lesson. You will need their permission first. Then, ensure they agree to your plan to include the testimonial in your teaching curriculum.

Testimonials during workshops and seminars

During workshops and seminars, you can use the coffee breaks for interviewing and recording reviews—it makes for an exciting and fun diversion.

Of course, you will need the following:

- A video camera or your computer web camera and microphone, or

- A microphone connected to a recording device for audio testimonials.

> **TIP**: The easiest and simplest method to help your students over their first embarrassment hurdle is to ask them a question they can easily respond to without too much thought. It eases the pressure and allows them to warm up. They are talking to you—not a camera or microphone.

Another advantage of recorded versus written testimonials is that they *sound* authentic because they are (seemingly) spontaneous and 'off-the-cuff'. The viewer or listener doesn't see how people read your question (or questions) beforehand. They only watch (or hear) how they describe your course, workshop or seminar.

The verbal testimonial

Defuse all writer's blocks by letting them understand they are not giving a testimonial *per se,* but are recounting their learning experience. Subsequent questions draw on their memories. As they talk and reminisce, their memories become spiced with vivid details. They recall personal details that refer only to their situation and provide that unique personal touch. It 'sounds' authentic to potential customers listening later.

Reluctant corporate customers

Why are corporate people reluctant customers when asked to give testimonials? How would business people, particularly customers higher up or at the top of the hierarchy chain, react to your request for a testimonial?

Experience shows that the higher the hierarchy, the more likely they will resist (for several reasons). Are there any measures we can use to get past this resistance?

Learning English as a second language is a typical example where business people may be worried about the impact of taking private courses in their careers.

- Unwilling to make public that they had a deficiency in their English skills

- Possible disclosure of confidential topics

- Unwilling to pass on an excellent resource by waiting for *your* available time slots—because they don't want to lose flexibility in their own personal time management.

Can we change the way executives respond to our requests?

Top corporate people are renowned for turning problems around. Frequently, they make disadvantages appear as advantages. We can emulate this technique by reframing our requests to help corporate leaders recognise there are no threats or dangers to their careers.

For example, executives taking private English lessons in the corporate world may think if this becomes known, they are admitting to having a deficit in English.

The *how*-steps to follow depend on the type of tuition we provide and why the customers are taking English lessons. Let's consider a couple of ideas to demonstrate.

Example of reframing questions from a negative point of view into a positive aspect

A person's natural tendency is to <u>avoid doing repetitive work wherever they can</u>. One can call these people *lazy*. That is quite definitely a **negative trait**.

However, it is possible to turn this around by reframing this negative trait and give it a **positive aspect**.

So, with this example, you could say that you have *a keen eye to spot where repetitive work can be optimised to save time and effort*.

Presenting business people with reasons for using English language teaching services

1. English **continuously changes vocabulary, catchphrases, trends, fads, and jargon** (e.g., law, finance, technology, engineering, environment, economics, politics, terrorism, and new lifestyles).

2. Understanding where corporate customers work and what global issues confront them in their daily business lives.

   Examples:

   a. **Global natural catastrophes**: energy and natural resources conservation, landscape gardening, recycling, *'Fridays for Future'* issues.

   b. **Medicinal and pharmaceutical services**: Global pandemics, home office, cybersecurity issues, artificial and human intelligence.

   c. Food industry, seafood processing, fisheries economics and maritime engineering

   d. Political issues, terrorism

   As you can see, the list is almost endless.

Tell them English can be emphasised as an ongoing business tool to ensure that:

- They **position themselves on the global business market**—renowned for their sharp communicative English speaking skills, *which private tuition enhances.*

- They constructively ensure their **power of freedom, independence and liberty** in English meetings and negotiations or when they give presentations.

And why?

1. Time reasons

Executives already live hectic lives; private tuition becomes an ongoing business tool to **save time**. When essential company accounts use specialised terminology and jargon, private tuition helps executives keep abreast of the ever-changing terminology.

- Private tuition saves time searching for and acquiring the terminology and jargon of their customer-specialised businesses

2. Location reasons

When they **live in a non-English speaking country**, they need to keep their English language level active (i.e., fluent). Private tuition allows them to discuss (current) world affairs and business, industrial, and technological trends.

- Working effectively in **cross-cultural communication** on **global issues**

- **Self-fulfilling enjoyment reasons**. Knowing they can converse in English on current world affairs, business, industrial, or technological trends with anyone they meet keeps the fun aspect alive.

3. Leadership objectives

Freelancers can derail corporate leaders' aversion to writing testimonials, such as encouraging **leadership objectives**. Lead your testimonial requests by asking these example questions:

- Is English as a communication language essential for the company?

- Does the company have employees striving to reach top positions within their company?

- Can you prompt executives to give company-specific reasons for encouraging their department personnel's 'can-do' attitudes?

- Could English tuition inspire internal company interest in self-development programmes (e.g., leadership qualities)?

The possibilities are manifold, yet each is unique to its own concept.

And interestingly, by default, when we help them recognise their successes and growing language skills, we also make them aware of *our contribution* to their progress.

Two kinds of testimonials

But what questions should we ask? What *kind* of questions can we ask our students to provoke memories of **past experiences** and/or help defuse wrong **perceptions**?

Logistical and experience-based testimonials

There is a difference between *logistical* and *experience-based testimonials*, which means we need to know the difference between them.

Quick overview of logistical testimonials

They request simple answers to a single (specific) *question* concerning the teaching business's basic service. (See p. 43.) These produce *short* testimonials.

Quick overview of experienced-based testimonials

The *experience-based* testimonial digs out the whole learning experience of our students. (See p. 79.)

Experience-based testimonials result in meaty content because they are incredibly rich in details. Such testimonials easily span 800 to 1500 words and read like book chapters. They describe the testimonial givers' feelings and experiences during your course, lessons, seminars, and workshops.

When to use *logistical* testimonials

Logistical testimonials enlighten readers on the sales page of your website or social media page and in your brochures. These resolve specific questions and allay any misgivings customers subconsciously set up to block (expensive) purchases.

Let's take, for example, that you are a one-person service. Business companies may perceive your service not as reliable compared to an education institute employing several teachers.

Of course, you cannot present your teaching service as having *a team of teachers* available. However, you can ask a company customer how your 'one-man service' compares to an educational institute employing several teaching employees or subcontracted freelancers. Such testimonials may give enough detail to present you as a reliable one-person teaching source.

A series of steps for your first *logistical* testimonial

1. Create a list of questions:

   When considering hiring you and your teaching service, create a list of questions potential students will think of. The first six to seven questions for your teaching field are generally easy to guess. However, you may wish to expand on these ideas and ask your students, friends, and colleagues for more ideas.

2. Ask your *current* students which one of these questions they would like to comment on as their testimonial?

3. Ask your student to prepare a testimonial based on this one question.

EXAMPLE (how to go about getting the first testimonial):

1. You are selling English language lessons for very young children. The most frequent question is about prices and whether the parents of the young child believe your price is far too expensive. Especially if children are *very young.*

2. You contact other past customers (parents with *very young children*) and ask them to describe whether the tuition you provided their children was worthwhile (price-performance ratio).

3. Should you ask several parents, you'll soon have a small series of testimonials dealing with this one question—the price question—that you can add to your website (or the social media pages you prefer to use and your brochures). These are not just providing proof of customer satisfaction. They've also discreetly answered one of the critical questions plaguing future customers and freelancers alike: *Is the price too high?*

What if you have other questions on your list? Besides the price question, have *parents* mentioned other questions?

If they do, and it is related to your question (here it is about the *price*), collect different and new testimonials to answer other **price-associated** questions as well. These can be added afterwards with their testimonials to your **supporting** proof where you need them (e.g., website, brochures).

TIP: Avoid references to prices and discounts

Future students and business customers will believe whatever is written in a testimonial. Whatever they see written—they will expect.

So, for example, when a price or a discount is mentioned, they will expect to receive the *same price and discount conditions* offered in the testimonial.

When to use *experience-based* testimonials

Experience-based testimonials are extremely handy as downloadable PDFs, video and audio files on the **sales page** of your website and social media pages.

Experience-based testimonials are intense stories that go far beyond the scope of a single, specific question.

These are the recounted memories of past customers describing particular *Aha!* moments and even points of despair. No one student explains these highs and lows exactly like another because they are full of emotions and are rich with specific details that only they can describe.

The written or recorded word-of-mouth experience of another customer is incredibly persuasive.

Experience-based testimonials are super useful when a modicum of effort to format the written testimonial attractively entices potential customers to read them. Potential customers read, skim and re-read the whole to catch the flavour of another person's fantastic experience with your teaching service.

How to get 'meaty' *experience-based* testimonials

By *meaty*, I am talking about testimonials that are chock-a-block full of details compared to boring, sterile one-liner testimonials.

One-liners do not have the depth to entertain or express emotions. They don't tell stories to potential future students sitting on the fence, dithering about whether to buy into your teaching service.

How do you get longer and meatier testimonials? By providing examples.

Provide new testimonial-givers with examples rich in detail and imagery as an example to develop their own structure. These examples cue them in advance to write longer and more detailed references purely based on the models you gave them, which are also written in great detail.

So, what do you have to do next?

Get that first 'meaty sample' testimonial.

TIP: Avoid lists in single-word, bullet-point-like lists (if possible)

Single words do not have any details. When the list is long, they cancel each other out.

For example, *this book is **informative, interesting to read, very perceptive, written friendly, is professional and easy to follow**.*

What can the next reader expect from such a list? Where are the details to show how informative? Why was it interesting to read? And so forth... When your student gives you one word, get them to explain.

The first 'meaty' *experience-based* testimonial

1. If you don't yet have written testimonials, pick up **the telephone** for your first one.

Why the telephone? Because telephoning is by far the easiest tool to use. Or you can use online platforms (*Zoom*, *Skype*, etc.) as they are natural alternatives.

However, we want to get that first testimonial. Online platforms mean additional steps are involved: email or telephone to organise the meeting, setting up the discussion, checking the audio/recording on both sides is functioning, etc.

---

2. Tell your students the call should only take eight to ten minutes of their time. In addition, you will record the testimonial. This will save them the trouble of writing one themselves from scratch. And, of course, you will transcribe the recording—a recording you will have made for this purpose and for this purpose only.

3. Let them know that written testimonials could take up to 50 minutes of their time to write. However, you will both only require a maximum of 10 minutes for a recorded verbal testimonial.

You'll most likely hear sighs of relief. This information often persuades them to say 'yes' to your request.

Interestingly, people speak at about three words a second. That is about 180 words/minute, which makes for 1,800 words in approximately 10 minutes. How great is that?

4. Either transcribe the recording yourself or pay for a transcription service.

5. Give a copy to your testimonial-giver to approve. If they wish for any changes, ensure they receive a copy of the changed testimonial.

6. Aim for five to ten testimonials.

TIP: Find out the *'before'* and *'after'* situations. (See p. 56.)

Aim to get the story (the emotions), not just a statement.

Emotions provide the authentic touch that makes for *interesting-to-read* testimonials.

Unexpected critical testimonials

You have your (first) testimonial—but oh dear! There is a critical comment in its middle.

Unexpected criticism

What if a testimonial includes complaints? Do you throw it away? No, of course not. You need to keep it for two reasons:

1. You use it as a working document to improve your lessons or workshop-seminars and your teaching service offers.

2. You keep it to balance good and 'bad' testimonials.

Strange as it may seem, if you *only* provide testimonials extolling your teaching service, potential customers could become suspicious of purely '5-star' reviews. However, customers are reassured when there is a balance of good testimonials against ones with some (light) critique. Furthermore, they will appreciate that your teaching business isn't hiding unpalatable truths when they read several sides to the story.

A so-called 'bad' testimonial will always appear at some point. However, these can be defused if you plan for them in advance. These may even be welcome suggestions.

How? They may detail improvements for your teaching service you may have overlooked. This generally happens when you ask your students for feedback on certain teaching aspects to present a complete picture of your teaching business and tuition.

Testimonials are associated with glowing praises

The problem is that people automatically connect the word 'testimonial' to 'glowing praises'. As a result, most of our efforts to elicit them become over-glowing reviews.

Unfortunately, these only *sugary-sweet* testimonials cause the opposite reaction to what you want to achieve as the freelancer of your teaching business. *Nobody* believes a person or service is *that* good.

A typical example of a sugary-sweet review is a person's curriculum vitae (CV).

So yes, you *should* plan to receive 'critical' testimonials as part of your marketing paraphernalia. Preparing for these in what I call *flipped* testimonials would be best.

Flipped testimonials are small diversions

Travelling by car, we learn about new locations and explore new ways to reach our destination when we follow 'blocked road diversion' signs. We'll happily follow the signs knowing we will be back on track to our original destination later.

In a similar manner, these diversions can be likened to a flipped classroom teaching technique. First, the teacher creates a diversion or an opposing statement (i.e., getting the class to approach new learning methods and/or rules). Then, before getting back *en route* (testimonial's aim), the teacher fulfils the teaching plan.

The advantage of using flipped testimonials

Where most testimonials begin and end with praise, a flipped testimonial starts by expressing doubts. A flipped testimonial starts in an unexpected direction.

Let's stop for a moment and retrace our intentions.

For several reasons, most people are sceptical about paying for *services*:

- Foremost, it's a commodity over which they have no control.

- Second, because qualification standards differ from country to country, customers question whether the freelancer can do a good job.

It's unfortunate, but most testimonials don't accommodate such doubts. And yet, most people use flipped testimonial techniques to describe their daily experiences. That is, they start with a bit of doubt. So, for example, we say things like:

- *Do you remember that posh restaurant we saw? We thought it would be terribly expensive, but we were quite surprised to find out their prices are really reasonable.*

- *Do you recall Jason's little restaurant under the bridge? The one where the food was great, but the waitresses were awful? Well, we went there the other day expecting the worse. But the owner has got new waitresses, and the lunch turned out to be fantastic.*

- *Remember that yoga school where Joan twisted her back in class and had to call the doctor? Well, now the yoga school has changed its syllabus by concentrating on 'injury-free yoga lessons.'*

When testimonials begin with a (tiny) bit of doubt, they make it sound believable. And authentic. While collecting testimonials, you need to integrate a flipped testimonial technique into your logistical and experience-based testimonials.

Testimonial mistakes

Mixing up feedback with testimonials

Keep testimonials and feedback separate. The questions are similar, but the reasons fulfil different purposes.

- The **testimonial** answers questions potential customers have lurking in their subconscious

- The **feedback** (or critical assessments) pinpoint areas for improvement in your teaching service

Asking for testimonials is not the same as asking for flipped testimonial *appraisals*. A testimonial is about getting proof (and praise) of your tuition, but you can also use it as feedback.

Yet mixing testimonials and feedback can cause both you and your student confusion. So, what is the difference between testimonials and feedback?

- When your customer heaps you with lavish praise about your tuition—when you feel like a cat bathed in cream—that's a testimonial.

- When students tell you how to tighten up your work processes or point out typos or possibly other mistakes in your teaching materials—that's feedback.

With feedback, you shape and design your lessons to fit students' requirements. Feedback gives you a deep insight into your teaching service you cannot get elsewhere.

Overall, most students want to be helpful. Still, when critical issues overtake praise, it's easy to become disillusioned with the entire process (collecting testimonials). It is not what you envisioned. At the same time, it's easy to overlook your students' feelings. It can be that *they* are not happy either. They genuinely wanted to give you *a lot more* praise instead of the criticism they've just revealed.

> You will intuitively know whether a student is just plain nasty or not succeeding to get their point across without sounding harsh.

Two for the price of one—critical appraisals and testimonials

The solution lies in what questions are asked at the time of the request and in which order.

One sound strategy is to start with the critical appraisals first. This allows your student to get their (unlovable) feedback out of their system. Afterwards, they will be more than happy to answer your testimonial-related questions.

Having had the chance to get issues out of their system and clear the atmosphere, they will want to balance all those critical statements with praise.

So let them.

You'll find the testimonial that follows rewarding. The praise becomes more colourful and much more detailed. But, of course, the whole relies upon the order in which you ask the questions.

For example:

1. *What parts of the course (lessons) could be improved?* **(feedback)**

2. *What suggestions or ideas do you have?* **(feedback)**

Once they have presented their feedback, you slowly lead your customers into giving their positive appraisals. Once the feedback is done and dusted, you can turn your questions into testimonial-related **(appraisal)** questions.

3. *Have you taken part in other < ... > courses?*

4. *What is your overall impression of the course (lessons) in comparison?* [in response to 3. above]

5. *What parts did you enjoy most?*

6. *How far have you reached your learning aim (personal business or private objectives)?*

Have you noticed how these steps reveal your student's *'before'* and *'after'* experience? Indeed, the testimonial aims to establish **the purpose** behind your student's *'before'* and *'after'* experiences with your teaching service. (See p. 24.)

The BEFOREs and AFTERs are critical for your testimonial

Assist your students in realising that they're not just giving a testimonial *per se*. They are merely recounting their *'before'* and *'after'* situations. You are searching for **stories describing their experience.**

It is necessary to avoid monosyllabic answers and quick one-liners. For example:

Why did you decide to attend the course (lessons)?

- *Because my boss said I had to.*
- *Because I decided to improve my English.*

With the tiniest bit of extra effort (you change the question slightly), you prompt them to give you their story.

EXAMPLES:

[before experience]:

1. *What was your first reaction when a colleague told you about my course (lessons)?*

Alternatively, if they stumbled across your website or social media page:

2. *What were you hoping to achieve when you found my website (a colleague told you about my courses)?*

3. *What was your situation* [personal or career situation] *before attending the course (lessons)?*

[after experience]:

4. *Now that you've taken part in the course (lessons), how has the course (lessons) helped you?*

5. *Does a specific event or learning achievement come to mind?*

6. *Would you recommend the course (lessons) to someone else? If so, why?*

Testimonials—but I forgot to ask!

We're human beings, and forgetfulness can be problematic if we consistently forget to ask for them. Or when we remember, it's too late.

Far too often, students never send in their promised testimonials. And when they do, it's still a lost opportunity for reviews or discussions (when it's fresh in their minds) about personal changes while speaking directly to your students.

Is there a reliable way to avoid this forgetfulness? Yes! For example, by using:

1. Templates

Prepare lesson or seminar templates with highlighted 'comment' reminders. Insert the questions you'd like to ask on your different testimonial templates (at the beginning, during, and end of a series of lessons, courses or workshop-seminar).

2. Post-It stickers

If you haven't prepared template plans, stick colourful Post-Its on your lesson worksheets. These are wonderful reminders (provided you remember to put them there). The colour catches your eye each time you refer to your lesson plan.

3. Highlighting text on worksheets

Add and highlight reminder notes on student worksheets, workshop-seminar documents or presentation handouts.

Getting testimonials in advance

(For your lessons, courses and workshop-seminars)

Advanced reviews (testimonials) are *everywhere*. For example, computer games extolling new games have advanced reviews. New cinema films and books also have them. The common denominator is that they are *all* available in advance. So why not your teaching service, too?

When you've still to get a student (or create a teaching product)

'This is all very well, but I haven't got a student yet!' you might be thinking. It's easy to believe (and most do) you can only get testimonials once you've taught several students or have run a couple of workshops and seminars.

That's not true.

You can get testimonials even *before* your lessons and courses start and, of course, while they are **still in progress**.

The testimonial process can start earlier than you'd expect

The three situations below are where teaching freelancers struggle to get testimonials:

1. Freelancers are just **beginning their teaching careers** and don't yet have any students or business customers

2. Their students or business customers **haven't yet completed their course or workshop**

3. **Teaching products (leverage[5]):** They don't have a teaching material product available yet, or they are still work-in-progress (WIP) projects

Three specific points to get testimonials

Most of us wait until a course (workshop-seminar) has finished before asking for testimonials. It's a commendably good idea. But getting your customer to give you one without warning them in advance makes it much harder for the freelancer to get one.

Also, you are not restricted to 'end-of-the-course' testimonials. There are easier (and earlier) points when you can ask for a testimonial.

---

[5] See *Book 1 Pricing Matters* for the *Three-pillar concept*

1. End Testimonials (the classic)

You get these testimonials at the end, not after the course or workshop-seminar, but at their conclusion. Customers can do these small, extra assignments (or should do) as part of their last exercise or as part of an additional assignment outside the class or workshop-seminar room.

Waiting until *afterwards,* when customers have left the room or the course, will cause you (almost) insurmountable hurdles in getting your testimonials.

2. In-Progress Testimonials

These are great for long courses and workshop-seminars running over several days/weeks.

The danger here is that when students are asked for a testimonial too late, they often forget how they felt at the start of their tuition. This destroys all your hopes for *'before'* and *'after'* situations.

But the real benefit of in-progress testimonials is that they create great opportunities for when your courses and teaching materials are so new that they are incomplete. For example, typical instances are:

- When your first-ever workshop is still in progress
- Your student has only just started taking your lessons

In-progress testimonials focus on single points, benefits, wishes, or recently completed features.

3. Initial Testimonials

You inform students of your need for testimonials at the start of your working relationship. Your request should be stated during your first STUDENT interview[6] with your future student. That is:

- Once you have established their ultimate aim in taking your course and why they need to learn

- Once they have hired you as their private instructor

How *initial* and *in-progress* testimonials work

The first contact with the new student or business customer is the best time to ask whether they would give you a testimonial. Have them agree to provide a testimonial immediately when they enrol for your course or lessons, the *initial testimonial* stage.

> NOTE: An *initial testimonial* also works for **teaching products**.

The INITIAL testimonial

You are, in fact, setting up your position *in advance*. It's a critical step, especially when starting your teaching business and you haven't yet established your reputation.

---

[6] See *Book 1 Pricing Matters* (a homestudy course on all pricing and financial matters for teaching freelancers) and the chapter detailing how to run *The STUDENT interview*

This agreement is a big psychological boost in getting your testimonial—even *before* the course begins. When someone has agreed to give you a testimonial, the chances are they will honour their agreement.

With your *first* live lesson, workshop, or seminar, let the students or business customers know you are keen to receive feedback and testimonials. People *do* expect to be asked for one at the end of their course, but—please note—they are usually quite willing to give feedback **much earlier**.

You'll notice that they often want to balance their critical assessments with praise for what has already impressed or changed things for them.

This is your chance for a testimonial.

First, ask them to elaborate on the point they've just mentioned (which they generally do). That elaboration is your testimonial.

The IN-PROGRESS testimonial

You follow up *initial* testimonials with *in-progress* testimonials. It's natural to follow up by requesting another at the end of the course or workshop, the *end* testimonial.

Many customers are happy to give you an *in-progress* testimonial. This is when, at an appropriate point during your course (workshop-seminar), you ask them for one or two areas they felt were already useful or valuable for them.

For example, if you are giving workshop-seminars, you could ask them what they liked in the section covering « ... ».

Different approaches when asking for testimonials

The point to digest is to set up your testimonial-getting strategy in advance. Below are three examples:

- *Will you be happy to give a testimonial at « ... » (a specific time) or after « ... » (a workshop-seminar benchmark)?*

- *We might not have finished the course (workshop-seminar) yet, but would you be happy to cover a point that gave you some insight or a learning point? [to « ... »]*

- *Here's an example of a testimonial another student gave to help you see the kind of testimonial you can give. Would you be happy to tell me about « ... » in about half an hour?*

Asking for testimonials

Asking for LESSON testimonials (open-end)

1. with FACE-TO-FACE students

How do you ask for LESSON testimonials with face-to-face (new *and* ongoing) students?

The precise moment to request a testimonial depends on your students. For example, you *could* spend one of your lessons getting a testimonial. However, your students *could* interpret this tactic as using up their time and money with no visible advantage (for the student).

One solution is to ensure your course includes several assignments, then embed the feedback and testimonial as part of the course structure. (See p. 67.)

The structure to follow is either an **initial**, an **in-progress** or an **end** testimonial (see p. 60).

2. **with ONLINE students** (As above: FACE-TO-FACE LESSON students)

Most of your online students will be adept on the computer. They are most likely to have accounts with *Zoom* or *Skype, Facebook, Twitter, Google docs,* etc.

- An excellent way to add to your collection of alternative testimonial formats is to ask your online students to leave a recorded one on your social media account.

- There is nothing to prevent you from asking for a traditionally written reference.

With **online courses:** one method could be to drip-feed your information (assignments, videos, audio, etc.) and then ask them for their '*biggest takeaway in learning*' after each task.

Alternatively, ask them to write in the comment box (or chat box) after each video or audio.

Asking for COURSE testimonials (set finish date)

with ONLINE students (see also p. 65)

How do you ask for COURSE testimonials from online students?

Ensure your course includes several assignments, then embed the feedback and testimonial as part of the course's assessments. When?

It depends on whether you implement an **initial, in-progress** or **end** testimonial (see p. 60). Planning for and including testimonials during the last course days may be possible as a feedback assignment. For example:

- Day 1—Post your feedback using one or more of the following questions as a guide

- Day 2—Post your experience of the course (testimonial) by using one or more of the accompanying questions as a guide

- Day 3—Give thanks and say goodbye to your group

Asking for WORKSHOP-SEMINAR testimonials

Again, you could spend some of the (live, face-to-face) workshop-seminar time getting testimonials.

However, your participants could construe this as using their 'workshop time' and protest. Yet if you wait until the workshop ends, everybody is too tired and has only one thought left—to go home. What now?

Here are two methods to help you get those coveted testimonials:

Method 1: Getting testimonials during breaks

Breaks are the small spaces of time just before the workshop begins or after the day's event (when it runs over several days), or during tea and coffee breaks. Breaks can be early in the mornings, during morning and afternoon coffee breaks, and during the hour-long lunch break.

How does it work?

- **Tools**: Tripod plus a good quality microphone (e.g., Rhode), or a mobile phone (e.g., Smartphone or a mobile capable of making short videos) and a notebook.

- **Preparation is the key:** It's going to be EXHAUSTING. Don't be afraid to ask one or two of your participants for the help you need. Someone to help keep the noise level down and somebody (or two) to help should things go wrong.

1. **Start with *recurring* clients first**

   Or *current* clients with whom you've established a good working relationship.

   Customers you already know are usually willing to help you. Maybe it's still too early to provide a testimonial about the workshop itself, but when you concentrate on a single element—their insights about their expectations and the atmosphere on their arrival—you can get the first testimonial.

   When customers have *already attended other workshops* you've given, they can compare your other workshops (if they've not yet given you a testimonial) with what they now expect to learn and/or have just learned in this new course or workshop-seminar.

2. **In-progress testimonials** (new *and* existing customers)

    a. Make sure your participants '*book*' the time slot for their testimonials. Reserving their time slot allows other participants to watch and observe the recording process. More importantly, they will see how other participants answer the questions.

    b. Ask your participants (one or two) questions on what has impressed or changed things for them during the course (workshop-seminar) and whether they can elaborate on that point.

Method 2: The learning scenario

One-day workshop-seminars require **'the end'** type of testimonials. However, get **'in-progress'** testimonials whenever possible when your workshop seminar runs over several days. At the end of a session (especially after a several-day workshop), ask participants to share their learning (of that day) and any observational insights they've experienced. Give one participant the microphone and request them to pass it on to the next participant willing to share their learning/insights.

What do you achieve with this technique?

1. It's a great way to help participants recall what they learned that day.

2. It's indirect feedback for you because it confirms (or not) whether the participants have recalled the most important teachings of the day.

3. When participants share their insights about your workshop in two to three minutes, you have an approximate 500-word testimonial. And best of all, it's part of the workshop and learning process.

TIP: The biggest frustration you will experience is an eager participant speaking without holding the microphone. As a result, all your attempts to have a clean recording of the workshop are thwarted, and you have extra work afterwards.

Plan for some 'penalty exercise' when this happens—something silly and humorous such as reciting a nursery rhyme, or catching and keeping a seminar mascot until the next person speaks before receiving the microphone.

Questions for LOGISTICAL testimonials

Six questions for logistical-based testimonials

How often should freelancers ask their students for testimonials?

- We need to ask different participants for testimonials when they enrol for your courses *and* several times *during* a course.

- We have to ask repeatedly for testimonials at regular intervals with our long-term and ongoing students.

Of course, our students can produce a testimonial without guidance from us. However, what happens when the testimonial-giver doesn't know what to write? Or has writer-block? Or has no time to consider what to write?

Add to this situation another minor problem of not wanting to broadcast how excellent our lessons and courses are compared to others—where we suddenly realise readers start raising their eyebrows or mentally backing off from the glowing praise. It would be much better if our potential customers didn't have to reach out for an extra-large pinch of salt.

Unfortunately, sustaining the success of your teaching business means you are left with no other alternative than to prepare helpful questions—*as a testimonial guide.*

We want to avoid our students becoming tired of writing the same old text written in most testimonials. No student likes or wants to give the same written testimonial over (and over) again. Likewise, we won't be happy about receiving their dutifully copied and pasted old testimonials.

You can avoid all this by giving them a new question or set of questions when the time arrives to prepare testimonials.

A question that the student hasn't yet answered, together with an example from another student. Or a set of new questions covering a different topic.

If you don't yet have a written testimonial model, ask the student to allow you to record their answer. *Remember, we get about 1,800 words in about 10 minutes because people talk at about three words a second.*

Six areas to kick-start a LOGISTICAL testimonial

First, the six core areas, then the different ways to ask your students the questions based on logistical reasons—those concerning the teaching business itself.

1. **Reasons for choosing the course (or workshop-seminar)**

2. **Decision approaches to taking the course**

3. **Requests on how to improve the course or seminar**

4. **Requests for stories about experiences and results of choosing the course**

5. **Giving advice to future participants**

6. **Anything else you want to say or add?**

1. Reasons for choosing the course (or workshop-seminar)

Choose ONE question to ask:

- What was your reason for taking this course (workshop-seminar)?

- What ultimately convinced you to purchase this particular course?

- Was there something that almost kept you from buying or enrolling for this course (workshop-seminar)? [If yes, what was it?]

- Have you done other courses with me? Will you sign up or consider signing up for another course (workshop-seminar)? Can you tell me why? (Why not?)

- What would have been the consequences if you hadn't attended the course (workshop-seminar)?

- What reason could have prevented you from enrolling in my course (workshop-seminar)?

- What advice would you give people considering this course (workshop-seminar)?

---

2. Decision approaches to taking the course

Choose ONE question to ask:

- Describe the processes you used to research and eliminate choices while choosing « teaching field » courses (workshop-seminar).

- What did you feel is a major risk of private tuition? And what would you now say to a person considering this course (workshop-seminar) who feels the same doubt you felt when deciding whether to enrol in this course?

- Can you tell me what questions you had to consider before enrolling in this course? Can you tell me why you chose my courses over other similar teaching courses?

- What training aspects (features) were you glad to see in this course? Why were these (features) necessary for you?

- What was the reason (or reasons) you felt confirmed you had made the right decision to attend this course (workshop-seminar)?

---

3. Requests on how to improve the course or seminar

Choose ONE question to ask:

- How can I improve the course (workshop-seminar) to be more helpful or enjoyable?

- What is your biggest problem or frustration in your life/business right now that can be (or could be) resolved by attending this course?

- What did you find especially useful in attending this course (workshop-seminar)?

- What specific course (workshop-seminar) module or topic interested you the most?

- Have you purchased other (similar) courses?

- If this course (workshop-seminar) could produce a specific, tangible result/outcome for you, what would that be?

---

4. Requests for stories about experiences and results of choosing the course

Choose ONE question to ask:

- Can you tell me your overall feeling about this course (workshop-seminar)?

- How did the course (workshop-seminar) help you? And personally? Did you achieve any particular learning aims? Or have you perhaps attained a professional purpose?

- How did the extra learning modules help? For example, « ... »?

- Can you think of three benefits that could interest other participants about this course (workshop-seminar)?

---

5. Giving advice to future participants

Choose ONE question to ask:

- What advice would you give to people who have never heard about my courses?

- Can you describe how this course (workshop-seminar) is taught to someone who has never attended one of my courses? (Teaching methodology, the instructor, etc.)

- Do you have any 'special' personal experiences you can recall, for example:

  The moment I understood « ... », it was a special moment for me because in the past « ... » happened and now « ... ».

- Can you describe what you think are unusual elements I've used in this course (workshop-seminar)? What were they, and how useful were they in helping the learning process?

- How would you describe what makes this course (workshop-seminar) unique? Special?

- How would you describe me as a teacher [trainer, coach]?

---

6. Anything else you want to say or add?

Example questions:

- Is there anything else you would like to say (to add)?

- Would you recommend this course (workshop-seminar)? If so, why?

As a reminder

Request permission from the giver of your testimonial to use it for your marketing purposes (e.g., promotional materials, social media page, website).

A photograph with a name has more influence (makes the written word more believable) than one without. (See About testimonial photos on p. 99.)

Request their permission to use their photo with their name, work position, and possibly the company's name. You will need their permission even when they are reposted from the original testimonial posted on a website or on some printed promotional prospect. Likewise, when they are transcribed from audio or video.

Questions for EXPERIENCE-based testimonials

---

17 experience-based testimonial questions

Yikes! Seventeen questions? Won't my students stare at me in disbelief when I present them with 17 questions during or at the end of a workshop?

Yes, they will think you've gone totally nutty and overboard with the whole testimonial thing.

But it's a different kettle of fish when you're in the middle of or have just completed a long course or 3-day workshop seminar. Your students won't be so bemused and will be more likely to accept your 17 questions because you've had time to develop a relationship with them. The same applies to students who have attended your face-to-face and online course over the last few weeks (or months).

Remind them they are *recording* their answers. Although it seems like a lot of questions, it only takes approximately 10 to 15 minutes of their time to answer them. Nonetheless, try to keep the questions as simple as possible.

But still... How does one prepare students to answer 17 questions all in one go?

It's a matter of ensuring you've worked out how to organise the stages and prepare yourself and your student *beforehand* to avoid everything disintegrating into digestive chaos.

TIP:

- Guide them into revealing your teaching methodologies.

- Guide your testimonial-giver to recognise their successes rather than reveal personal issues.

- And remember, you can always split the participant's testimonial into three recording sessions: The *Initial*, the *In-Progress* and the classic *End* testimonial.

Eating habits as we know them today

For example, French cuisine and table manners are primarily attributed to Catherine de' Medici's influence. She married King Henry II of France in 1533 and promptly changed French eating habits upon her arrival. As she was accompanied by her own servants, chefs, pâtissier and waiters, she immediately introduced unknown Italian foods, spices and recipes to the French kitchens.

It was customary in French courts to serve various food dishes all at once (tastebud chaos). The queen consort, Catherine de' Medici, changed this as well. She revolutionised how the French court served food by separating savoury foods from sweet dishes by declaring what dishes should be served at the table and when. Before she arrived in France, eating food by hand and a knife and spoon was customary. She organised the royal table's new place settings and decorations with a new cutlery tool—the three-pronged fork.

We will do the same. We shall separate our tasks into sections to avoid overwhelming our students.

1. **Send the questions to the students in advance and explain what is expected**

   Let's face it, nobody likes to be surprised with a list of 17 questions unannounced. However, it's important to send them this information in advance, irrespective of whether the testimonial will be done on the telephone, in person, or online. They must know they will be answering 17 questions.

At the same time, you need to explain how this helps you get more detailed (meaty) testimonials. If they ask, tell them that one-liner statements are useless for you and future students as they don't hold enough information.

If you suspect they will bulk at answering 17 questions, explain (by telephone or talk to them in person) before sending the questions. Then ask them if they would prefer to *record* their testimonial (i.e., while talking to

---

Various question examples using the student's 'overall course experience' as its focus

- **Experience**: before, during, and after completing the course

- **Elements of the course**: the group (and forum for online courses), teaching materials (presentation notes), any videos or audios used during the course or presentation.

- **Teaching methodology**: how it's taught, teacher response, peer-to-peer teaching, etc.

- **Comparison**: how does this course compare to others taken by our students in the past?

you on the phone). They would save time in writing and editing by just answering you.

2. **The questions should be grouped and related to one part of the course or a workshop section.**

    Determine *the purpose* (see p. 24; *the job to be done*) behind your testimonial. Then determine the focus of your testimonial questions bearing *the purpose* in mind. The focus is pivotal in assigning the parameters for the 17 questions to a single outcome. When necessary, rewrite the questions to encompass the purpose and your individual requirements.

3. **Send an example** (preferably several examples if you have them) **of testimonials** given by past students. This strategy sets up a mirror effect—a benchmark of what is expected.

The experienced-based questions

Without further ado, here are the seventeen questions.

> **NOTE:** *Adapt or change the example questions to fit your teaching service requirements:*

A. Experience—collecting reasons for taking the course, workshop or seminar

1. Can you tell me your reason for attending this course (workshop)?

2. Why did you choose *this* course over others on the market?

3. Describe how you felt at the beginning of the course. How did things change for you halfway into the course (workshop-seminar)?

4. And now? Can you describe how you feel *now*, towards the end of (at the end of) the course?

B. Elements of the course—collecting stories about experiences and results gained from taking this course (workshop-seminar)

Adapt or change the example questions to fit your teaching service:

5. What did you think the course would be like? Why wasn't it like that—and now you're glad it was different from what you initially thought?

6. What was the most challenging moment during the course (workshop-seminar)? How did you overcome it?

7. (a) *Face-to-face:* What is your opinion about the working relationship with the other students (class or workshop group)? Can you describe your experience?

(b) *Online:* Can you describe what you liked about working online in the forum (e.g., using *Zoom, Skype,* breakout rooms)? Was it a positive experience? Do you believe it has made a difference in your learning?

C. Collecting information about the teaching methodology

*Adapt or change the example questions to fit
your teaching service:*

8. How would you describe my teaching methods to a newcomer?

9. How would you describe me as the teacher (instructor, coach, mentor)?

10. Did you experience any *Aha!* moments? For example, can you tell me about a personal experience where it suddenly clicked, and you realised that it *'all makes sense now'*? Were there other special moments that stood out in your memory during the course?

D. Comparisons and advising future participants

*Adapt or change the example questions to fit
your teaching service:*

11. What challenges did you experience during the course? How did you overcome them?

12. What would you say are your big takeaways from attending this course? Can you tell me about them?

13. How did this course help you personally in your (career, hobby, personal reasons) goals?

14. Have you taken part in any of my other courses (workshop-seminars)?

15. Would you recommend this course? And why?

16. Would you consider enrolling in another of my courses?

17. What advice would you give to people who have never attended one of my courses?

E. Any other comments?

18. Would you like to add anything else?

F. For those occasions when you have extended a course

19. How useful did you find the extra classes? How helpful were they for you?

A hands-on example from one of my customers

EXAMPLE: 17-question testimonial

The example is an adapted (privacy reasons) recorded testimonial of an elderly German couple. I translated their answers from German into English.

1. **What was your main reason for attending this course?**

We wanted to learn English to speak to our daughter and our grandchildren living in Australia. They only speak English.

2. **What was the main reason you chose my course?**

We're no longer the youngest and wanted to be sure we could understand what our grandchildren were saying to us.

3. **Describe how you felt things had changed about midway into the course.**

At first, we must say that we still feel unsure of ourselves. But we noticed we could understand a part of what our grandchildren were telling us on Skype.

4. **Can you describe how you both feel now, towards the end of the course?**

Much better. And our self-confidence has risen a lot since our visit to see a live concert in Hamburg.

5. **What did you think the course would be like? Why wasn't it like what you thought it would be?**

We thought it would be like other courses: written exercises and newspaper articles. But we spoke all the time. That was very good.

6. **[Not asked—they were a married couple]**
7. **[Not asked—a married couple, private tuition]**
8. **How would you describe this course to a newcomer?**

You are always speaking—all the time. Janine asks one of us questions, and we have to answer them. At first, it was unnerving because we had so little English knowledge, and we were afraid to make mistakes. But Janine made it clear from the start that mistakes are the best way to learn, and we should make plenty of them.

English is spoken differently from written English. We didn't realise that at first. But it's true. Spoken English is not the same, and Janine is excellent in getting you to understand how it's spoken and how to understand spoken English.

9. **How would you describe me as the teacher?**

Friendly. We were surprised by how patient you are when we needed more time to practice. Sometimes we deliberately didn't understand—to find out how many more examples you could come up with. (laugh)

10. **Did you experience any *Aha!* moments? Were there other special moments that stood out in your memory during the course?**

Oh yes. The best moment was when we listened to a live concert in Hamburg. The conductor could only speak English, but we could almost understand everything he said. That was a real boost to our confidence.

11. **What kind of challenges did you experience during the course? How did you overcome them?**

It was realising that writing English is not written phonetically like in German. Sometimes it was a big surprise to see how the words were written in English. Not at all like spelling words in German.

12. **What would you say are the big takeaways from attending this course? Can you tell me about them?**

We're going to visit our daughter and grandchildren this summer!

13. **How did this course help you personally?**

By training our ears to understand English. If you know what is being said, you can better answer back.

14. **[Not asked—this was their first course]**
15. **Would you recommend this course? And why?**

We didn't believe we could ever learn to speak or even understand English. But you proved that we can.

16. **[Not asked—they had plans to go to Australia]**
17. **What advice would you give to people who have never attended one of my courses?**

Go for it. Don't give up on learning English. It's nothing like learning English back in the old school days, where we had to learn elbow-long lists of vocabulary and not know how to make a sentence from any of them. We don't remember speaking English in school either. School English was taught differently back then. In fact, we were excited to continue after the first lesson. It's unnerving at first, but Janine soon makes you realise it's all quite easy. She uses a different approach in how she teaches. It's strange at first, but you soon get used to it. Also, she only goes as fast as we can manage.

Random questions about testimonials

A teaching service should get written references from satisfied customers that can be used for student acquisition purposes, marketing and selling the teaching service. And yet—it's *sooo* easy to forget to ask your customers to write one.

A reminder about using testimonials (references)

It's just as easy to forget to ask for their permission to use their testimonials in your promotional materials on your website and social media page.

Remind yourself to always ask for AND to use references!

Saying 'thank you'

Should I offer incentives or gifts in exchange for testimonials? Yay, or nay?

One takes it for granted that everyone knows the etiquette of being polite, saying 'please' and 'thank you.' Saying 'thank you' to the testimonial-giver should be taken seriously. After all, they have given you their time. However, some people like to show appreciation and thanks with a gift. In this case, a surprise gift afterwards is acceptable.

It's a different scenario when testimonials are *bought*. Bought testimonials destroy its credibility—and possibly the freelancer's reputation. Gifts or incentives *can* be construed as 'bought.' Amazon's derision when reviews are paid for is one example.

Writer's block or a template?

A dedicated, written testimonial is unique and sincere but harbours potential problems. Even non-authors suffer from 'writer's block' when confronted with a blank sheet of paper or computer screen to write a dedicated reference. Plan ahead and prepare a template with a list of questions about your teaching to help jog the testimonial writer's memory.

Remember to forewarn the testimonial-giver before presenting them with your list of questions.

Avoid over-simplified testimonials

Avoid testimonials that only give MARKS (or indicate satisfaction levels with representative emoticons). Grades and emoticons don't produce the information needed. They simply do not answer all the *whats*, the *whys*, *where* and *when*, and of course, all the *how*-questions potential *new* students will ask when confronted with their subconscious questions.

Frequently Asked Questions (FAQs) and reviews

If you wonder whether testimonials are necessary, check the numerous examples on the Internet as FAQs or reviews of books (Amazon, Barnes and Noble, Bookshop, Kobo and others). What are they, if not templates of questions and answers customers have already asked?

Prepare and keep current for your specific business and marketing needs, a unique list of **Logistical and Experience-based Questions** focusing on your teaching service advertising requirements.

- Prepare a blank **Questionnaire** template in which you copy and paste specific *logistical* questions to ask your **preferred students** and business customers. (See the chapter on Terminology used in this book.)

- Prepare another blank **Questionnaire** template for your *experience-based* questions.

How many questions should you ask?

How many questions are the correct number to ask at any one time?

Based on my experience, this is how I would answer this question:

This depends on how long I have known the student or business customer, the length of the course or workshop-seminar, and the type of testimonial I want. For example, do I need a *logistical* testimonial? Or do I need an *experience-based* testimonial?

For first-time new customers, I'd choose to use a *logistical* testimonial. New students don't know me or my teaching methodologies. They need evidence to convince them about the quality of education I give. In this situation, I would only need two or three questions. However, I have also mixed in a *'before'* and *'after'* experience question for more interesting responses in the past.

If I were looking for meaty, *experience-based* testimonials, I'd ask most (if not all) of the 17 questions. These are best given in audio or video format and then later transcribed.

Sometimes, I have had to split the 17 questions into different time slots before getting a complete testimonial. So, for example, I'd begin with three to six questions. Then in a different time slot (either in another lesson or on another day in a workshop), I'd ask the same student if we could continue and finish the testimonial recording. Usually, they agree, so I ask the next three questions. Interestingly, and depending on the student and the relationship with them I've developed during the course, I can often ask them *all* the remaining questions.

Should clients be informed in advance?

Should you tell clients in advance that you will request a testimonial later?

The information gives your students time to digest your request. Try to frame your request with an invitation to provide a list of possible questions if you believe your new student will shudder at the thought of answering 17 questions off the cuff. Let them know it will be a ca. 10-minute recording and transcribed later. This way, the pressure on the student relaxes.

Alternatively, you can insert the feedback and testimonial into their course.

With more amenable students, you can say something along these lines: *Would you agree to write a testimonial for me in a few months* (weeks, days) *from now—once you feel that you have significantly improved (or reached) your* « the agreed-upon benchmark »?

Should you inform clients in advance?

Why send out the questions in advance? Here are a couple of advantages and disadvantages to consider.

- People can prepare their answers better. When people cannot prepare, they don't have enough time to think about their answers. The person may feel that their responses could be more supportive—to you as their teacher. One reason is hindsight. They think they could have explained better or provided better and more illustrating examples.

  Such negative thoughts may cost future testimonials from the same person should they enrol in another of your courses or workshops.

- Ask them what format they prefer to give their testimonial (e.g., audio, video, written). Describe the interview as similar to taking part in a short conversation.

- When people prefer to *write* their testimonials, they may procrastinate at the sheer magnitude of the task.

  First, they must think of an answer to the question, write the testimonial, and then edit their answers. That task can take up to 45 minutes of their time. (See p. 47.)

- If they choose videos, take the time to coach them to look straight into the camera (as if they are talking to you face-to-face).

- A video recording can sound scripted. It's also possible that the person may keep looking down at their written notes while taking video testimonials. There will also be fewer *ahs* and *ums* to edit from your recordings.

What is the correct length for testimonials?

How *long* a testimonial should be is like asking how long a piece of string is. The length isn't important. There are short ones, long ones, and even *veerry* long ones. You can use all of them in whole (or in part). The only necessity is that they follow *the purpose* and must fit the determined requirements for your website, social media pages, and promotional materials.

Can I change the order or *structure* of a testimonial?

1. It's unnecessary to ask the questions in the correct order. Move the questions into an order that best fits the focus of what you want to be described. In fact, your student may choose to answer the questions in a completely different order. That's okay, too.

2. Testimonials can (generally) be used verbatim—as they are. However, sometimes you might find a lot of not-so-interesting pieces burying golden nuggets. Then it's okay to bring those golden nuggets closer to the top where they catch the reader's eye or display them as excerpts or quotes on your website.

3. You can edit and format testimonials to find your business's best impression and story. Readers considering enrolling in your courses want something digestible, helpful, easy to read and not long, full of fluff, meandering pages of text.

   Please remember to send the revised testimonial back to the student for any changes and their approval.

This brings us to ask the following question...

Is it okay to *edit* testimonials?

Should you edit the responses to be more concise while transcribing an audio recording? Sometimes a student can go completely off track before I can bring us back to the questions.

It is all right to use only one line of their testimonial if that is all you need. It's also okay if you use only one or two paragraphs. However, if you are changing the meaning (the context), please send a copy to the student for their review. They must have the chance to agree with your altered version.

When students speak in their mother tongue

Suppose you teach languages, and your website or social media pages are written in English. In that case, translate your testimonials.

Most of my freelancing career was in Germany. My students and business customers were German speakers. The testimonials were given in German, and I had to translate them. So, yes, I agree that this is a form of editing.

What if the person who hires you is not the student?

The two most common situations are company personnel departments and children's parents (or guardians).

Human Resources (HR) people hiring on behalf of their companies

Depending on the relationship you have developed with the company students, you may request both *logistical* and *experience-based* testimonials from them.

- *Logistical* testimonials are generally the more acceptable format for HR people.

Parents and guardians of children

You can weave both the child (or children) and their parents (or guardians) into one testimonial. Once you have the responsible person's permission, I would ask for the children's testimonials since they are the ones who have benefited the most.

For example, you can ask children:

- *What were **their** worries?* (i.e., before they met you)

- *What do **they** think were **their parents' (guardians')** reasons for bringing them to your course?*

- *How **they** feel now about **their own** learning success*

- *What do **they** think **their parents (guardians)** feel about **their** progress?* (i.e., today)

Afterwards, ask the parents or guardians for an additional testimonial.

About testimonial photos

Let's be clear about the advantages and disadvantages of using photos with testimonials.

Most photos on the Internet are not identifiable. Their faces are obscured by hats or sunglasses. Or they are either turned away from the camera or not looking directly into it. As teaching freelancers trying to gain new students, such photos won't create feelings of **trust**. The opposite happens.

Potential new students may laugh, but more worrying is that they wonder why the person is secretive or whether they have a disfigurement they want to be hidden.

1. Photos generate creditability for the testimonial itself. It creates credibility for the writer because the person is real rather than a picture of a baby, cat, dog, or cartoon. The photos represent the writer himself or herself.

2. They also create credibility for your teaching service because readers look at the photos as they read. They compare the face in the picture to get a feel for the person who wrote the review. It won't bother them whether they see them reposted from the written testimonial on a website, on some printed promotional prospect, or whether they were transcribed from audio or video. They gain confidence by seeing a face accompanying the written or transcribed wording.

3. Specifically, authentic photos help potential customers gain trust in your teaching service. Future clients may never enrol in your course when testimonials are written by a baby, cat or dog, or some other cartoon.

Getting clients to reveal their names

Some professions (e.g., law and medical) and corporate top hierarchical positions prefer not to give testimonials. And if they provide you with one, resist having their names or photos displayed. So it's (almost) impossible to get any from these professions.

How can we get such clients to include their names if they'd prefer not to?

For a start, you will be better served by avoiding the trigger word 'testimonial'. In situations such as these, names are inconsequential.

What you need are *case studies* (of their 'successes') either as recorded audios or written (not videos for obvious reasons). If the case study is full of professionally used terminology, it suffices to build credibility.

Be upfront and truthful as you explain why you need their testimonial. Ask them (each reluctant person) to let you have a successful case study—without divulging their names.

Case study successes replace testimonials because:

- Legal situations will be obvious to people working in the same profession

- Portrayed illnesses and treatments will also be obvious to others working in medical fields

Using portrayed anonymous case studies as examples give an additional future payoff. They act as an encouragement to persuade future case study givers to present new success stories.

TIP: Put a note at the top of your website or social media page

For example:

These case studies have no names, photos or identification of any kind because my customers value their privacy.

When you read about their successes, you will see that these situations may mirror your current situation. See how they resolved their issues.

Terminology used in this book

1. The 'Preferred Student Profile' concept

The **preferred student** is a concept in which we isolate a single student to represent all our *future* students—all the **Sallys** living in the world.

The **preferred student** is NOT a favourite student. These students are chosen from previous lessons or workshop-seminars that have run exceptionally well, with good learning/training results for both the student and the freelancer concerned.

The **preferred student profile** *document* results from an interview between freelancers and their chosen student who becomes their '**preferred student profile**'.

The goal is to achieve a stream of *better-quality* students, i.e., students we prefer teaching the most.

The '**preferred student profile**' concept is described in my second book: *The Ultimate Guide to Teaching Niches*.

2. WIIFM (What's in it for me?)

WIIFM is about purchasing habits. All buyers instinctively follow ingrained habits when they pay out hard-earned cash for a purchase that solves *their* problem or resolves *their* immediate need. When their WIIFM criteria are fulfilled—they will buy. When their WIIFM criteria are not fulfilled—they won't buy.

You can find WIIFM examples and explanations in my books: *The Teacher's Guide to Pricing Matters* and *The Ultimate Guide to Teaching Niches*.

3. Three-year death cycle of a teaching service

Teaching businesses fail due to cash flow problems—they have insufficient cash to cover their current liabilities. Lack of money chokes many teaching services and is one condition that leads to the premature death of a teaching service business within a three-year cycle. My first book and Homestudy Course, *The Teacher's Guide to Pricing Matters*, describes how to prevent this from happening.

Did You Find This Book Helpful?

Reviews are the heart and soul of a book's success. Only a good list of reviews encourages our colleagues to find it.

You can make an enormous difference. Because when you write a review, you'll be helping friends and colleagues discover useful books that help them grow their teaching business. And you will help authors—including myself—to keep writing them. Readers will often pass up a book no matter how interesting or great the cover sounds. Those stars and a few words have a huge impact.

This book will only be read if you tell readers about it. It would mean so much to me if you shared your view. It takes only a minute or two to leave an honest review at your preferred book retailer.

Your recommendation would help friends and colleagues decide which books to spend their time and money on.

Thank you in advance.

Janine

www.braymueller.com

About the Author

Teaching English has been my business and passion. I've been freelancing for around thirty years.

Today, I am semi-retired and wish to write a series of books giving practical marketing and business advice for teaching freelancers. I plan my books to help colleagues find students and earn enough to live from their profession.

I have worked in the Sales and Marketing departments in Belgium and Germany and completed two terms as a voluntary IATEFL Executive Marketing Committee member. I believe marketing was the key to helping me thrive in the freelance English language teaching market. Marketing helped me avoid the **three-year death cycle of most freelance teaching businesses**[7].

Meanwhile, I have been published in several language-teaching magazines. Please get in touch if you have questions.

---

[7] Teaching businesses fail due to cash flow problems—they have insufficient cash to cover their current liabilities. Lack of money chokes many teaching services within a three-year cycle and is one condition that leads to the premature death of a teaching service business. My first book, *The Teacher's Guide to Pricing Matters*, describes what you can do to prevent this happening.

HOW TO CONNECT WITH ME

Website

Entrepreneurial Freelance Teachers

@

www.ft-training.com

Author website

@

www.braymueller.com

Facebook

www.facebook.com/FTTraining

LinkedIn

www.linkedin.com/company/freelance-teachers---training/

Other Books Written by Janine Bray-Mueller

www.braymueller.com

Book 1: The Teacher's Guide to Pricing Matters

Quality Teaching Has Its Price—*What can I charge students?* A **Home Study Course** for freelancers to determine what to charge. Most freelancers who rely on *'the going rates'* continuously undercharge their teaching fees. Now they can work out an acceptable pricing rate commensurate with their skills and experience.

Book 2: The Ultimate Guide to Teaching Niches

Stand out in a crowded teaching market and find a steady stream of students—*How do you attract a constant flow of new students on the global teaching market?* What you don't need are theoretical discussions about niches and specialising. Instead, you need a practical, hands-on system that works.

Book 3: Tell me... What Do You Teach?

Marketing your teaching business to attract new customers *The importance of being different.* When you know how to teach but don't know what to write in your promotional materials, you can't tell your students what they gain by attending your courses. **They won't come**! Create a spotlight for your teaching business and catch the attention of new customers.

—QUICK READS SERIES FOR BUSY FREELANCERS —

Guidelines for Teaching Contracts

What happens to your teaching business when students don't pay or don't pay on time? *There aren't any rules unless you put them into place yourself.* Set the rules at the first meeting because a freelance teacher's income is jeopardised when they are not paid on time and their bills cannot be paid. And that is why you should always set payment rules from the outset. A regular income—a steady cash flow—keeps your teaching business alive. Remember, 80 per cent of businesses fail because they run out of money.